Thought

Talk

Kay Drummond

Copyright © 2016 Kay Drummond

All rights reserved.

Revised Edition

ISBN: - 0473359545

ISBN-13: **978-0-473-35954-6**

DEDICATION

To my husband for reminding me that the world is not going to swing off its axis because I have a problem. This puts things into perspective for me.

To my two children who let me know they love me.

CONTENTS

1	Single Thought	1
2	Fear of Failure	6
3	Inner Self	10
4	Negative Thinking	13
5	Take Control	23
6	Attitude	29
7	Create Your Future	35
8	Self Love	40
9	Personal Responsibility	46
10	Inner Change	51
11	Success in Failure	57
12	Stay Determined	64
13	Choices	70
14	Positive Thought Pattern	76
15	Motivation	83
16	You hold the Power	91

Your Thoughts Make Your Reality

Choose Them Wisely

1

A SINGLE THOUGHT

Everything you do starts with a single thought. When you aren't happy in your life, it's because your thoughts aren't the right thoughts. Thoughts can bring happiness into your life or they can bring sadness. What is amazing is that you are in charge of these thoughts; no one else can have them for you. So what will you do? Will you stay with the thoughts that make you unhappy or will you change your mindset and bring in those happy, positive thoughts?

Did you know, when you use your mind properly, you can make things happen, you can change your life. Wow, imagine that. Powerful stuff don't you think! Do you really appreciate just how powerful that mind of yours is, I wonder?

So many of us do the same thing day in and day

out. Our lives pass us by and we don't really make any plans to accomplish our dreams.

We tend to get stuck in our own little rut, or is it a comfort zone? Whichever it is, some of us just don't seem to make the effort to change our life to the way we want it.

How do you change the things in your life that you aren't really happy about? You need to have a strong will, determined attitude, and a positive mindset.

Thoughts are very powerful. When you believe you can, then you can. The power of the mind is incredible. You will be able to use your thoughts in the same way to have the lifestyle you desire. We all have this inner power that creates these moments, when we know exactly what we need to do

You may believe it isn't possible to make significant changes in your life, but it is. You can make these changes with the proper use of your thoughts.

Your thoughts influence you in everything. Your mind, your decisions, your expectations, your sense of humor, things you do, what you say, in fact everything is the result of your thoughts. You are the result of your thoughts. If you are not happy with how you are, change your thought pattern by being positive.

Still have doubts? You take time each day to take care of your body, your health and your appearance, so how about taking care of your inner self? Why not take a few minutes each day to build up your mind with positive self talk.

You are is the result of what you have told yourself over the years. So, what do you say? Do you tell yourself 'I am hopeless', 'I am useless at that', 'I'll never get it right'. Speaking like this will affect your confidence and could be the cause of bringing unhappiness in your life. Why not become your own best friend? You will find things happen much easier when you like yourself., and way to achieve this is through your self talk. Start to praise yourself today! Tell yourself how wonderful, confident, strong, capable, you are - plus anything else you want to become!

If there are things you want to do in your life and you don't seem to be getting anywhere it could be because you don't look on yourself as your best friend. It's important to like 'you'. Know that you are a person of value. Work on how you see yourself. Realize that you have many talents and tell yourself how you want to be.

Is there is something in your life you want to do but don't feel confident about? Start to tell yourself that you are capable and that you can do it. Really believe this and keep your thoughts positive.

Try not to let any negative thoughts creep into your mind. I know this isn't always easy. Maybe you have spent years telling yourself that you can't do things. When you really want to achieve at something, you have to tell yourself you can.

When your self talk is negative it will stop you achieving your dream. You have to believe that you are capable. Negative self talk will not win the day! Positive self talk will. When you believe you can, you will be capable of realizing your dream. Tell yourself how great you are. Try to realize your own importance and that no one is better than you. To like yourself is a powerful boost that will help you to build confidence and give the power you need to strive forward in whatever way you want.

When you really like yourself, and not just a little bit, you will surprised by what you can achieve! Don't take my word for it though, start talking that positive self talk and wait for the fantastic person you are to emerge. Once this happens start to make that dream a reality.

2

FEAR OF FAILURE

You can achieve everything your heart desires. This may sound too good to be true, and perhaps difficult to accept but it is true, and often the only thing that is stopping this achievement is yourself.

How many times in the past have you tried to do something, but you've done it half heartily because you really believe that you can't do it?

Why is this, I wonder? Often it's because of fear of failure. We set ourselves up with fearful thoughts that defeat what we want to do before we even try. Why do we do this to ourselves?

Do you listen to people who say you are hopeless, that you always try things and yet you never succeed. This is very demoralizing isn't it, and wont help you to get where you want. It's important that you find within yourself the courage to do what it is that you want to do. Search within yourself, for the answer is there waiting for you. You have to trust and believe in yourself, and know that if you really, really try you will be able to succeed. Unless you try how can you ever hope to do what it is that you want to do?

Fearful thoughts will hold you back. To get rid of fear you have to stop feeding your mind negative information. It's these thoughts that bring anxiety, and then, because you accept them into your mind, you instantly limit your ability. When you dismiss the thought and refuse to accept it, you will feel better within yourself.

When you think you can't do something then this is what happens. When you trust yourself and believe you can, you will improve your confidence, because the more often you talk in a confident way the stronger you will feel.

You have the ability to alter the way you are. Once you believe this, you can use your thoughts to change. The more you tell yourself about how capable you are, the sooner you'll become this way.

Strong confident self talk is essential. When you hear your thoughts becoming anxious, try to replace them with positive information. Don't let them take hold in your mind. You can choose to change your thoughts into something you want to hear.

When you feel scared try to ignore the thoughts, and change them into positive words. Tell yourself words such as 'I am not afraid' or 'I am a brave confident person', anything that will take your mind away from what scares you.

Why not attempt something that in the past you wouldn't have tried because you thought you would fail. Tell yourself that you can and will do it this time, and then stay determined, and try until you succeed.

Stay as confident as you can throughout your day. Replace any anxious thoughts that try to creep inside your mind, with positive information, and don't listen to anyone who tells you negative things about yourself.

Remember, your thoughts make you the way you are, decide today to be unafraid!

3

INNER SELF

Often, life throws up various difficulties, each one seems harder than the one before. When you feel you aren't coping, everything accumulates, one on top of the other. No matter how hard you try, how many times you try to lift your head above the worries that are happening in your life, nothing seems to go right.

People say everything happens for a reason. No doubt you ask yourself why on earth would you choose to go through all this stuff. One way of dealing with your problems is to take a look at your life. What are you doing? Why you are doing it? Once you accept that you really do want to change, you have taken the first major step to improve yourself.

It's easy for me to tell you that you hold the key to

your life, the key to bettering your circumstances. You might tell me that you have tried, but nothing works, no matter what you do, there is always something or someone that holds you back. One of the biggest obstacles you encounter is you! You have the ability to be the way you want. When you don't believe you are capable this stops you from being the best you can. The barrier to change in your life are the negative thoughts you have about yourself. Remember, your thoughts make you how you are.

You are unique and special, yet you may go through life unaware of this. Unaware of talents you may have. Are you uncertain as to how you can begin to become this unique and special person?

You first have to change the way you feel about yourself., work on the inner self. At this point in your life the inner you may be telling you that you are useless, unimportant, not capable, ugly, or unlovable. The inner you doesn't know any better because this is what your own thoughts have told it. Your self talk is a vital ingredient in becoming the 'real you'. Make your self talk positive. Every time you think you are not capable, turn that thought round. Tell yourself 'I am capable'.

The way you believe you are, is how you will be. When you are not the way you want to be you have the power and the ability to change. You do this by changing the thoughts you have.

What do you choose to believe? What do you want to believe about yourself? At this point, you may be at a low ebb and yet, for some reason, you have picked up this book. Why was this? I believe some things are meant to be. I also believe that I may be able to help you, but only you if you want to be helped, and this choice is yours.

4

NEGATIVE THINKING

Why is everyone better than me? Is this a thought you have? Why is it that you feel this way? The truth is that no one is better than you, but because you don't believe this, your negative thoughts have sunk deep into your mind and you believe that, yes, everyone is better than you.

When did you first start to doubt yourself? Did you have a sister or brother who was praised for being clever, or being pretty. Did no one pay you compliments, and so you felt insecure or unimportant. Maybe as you were growing into adulthood you were picked on by people you thought were friends Perhaps you longed to be like they were, and so you put up with the hurt feelings, even though you were crying inside from the pain their cruel words caused, because you thought that in the end they would accept you?

Did the partner of your dreams come into your life, only to let you down with cruel words or actions. Were you deflated with no praise, no kind words, just taken for granted and expected to do things without ever being thanked?

Nobody is better than you. You are great, you are special, you are worthwhile. However, unless you can accept this as true, you will find it difficult to change. Everyone has freedom of choice. Why not choose to pick up the pieces, and start thinking positively. Starting today decide you can be a success.

What you believe has shaped the way you are, so why not change the negative thoughts you have? Decide to day to believe in yourself and become the great individual that you long to be.

It may not be easy. You may have years of negative thinking to contend with, but when you stay positive in your effort to change your thoughts, you will slowly but surely begin to improve. No one can do this for you because your beliefs are your own, and only you can choose to change them. When you stay strong and determined you will succeed - the choice is yours.

Sometimes, everything will seem to have got an upper hand everything has gone negative, when you so wanted to stay positive. This is normal; it doesn't mean you can't change because you have lapsed back into a negative pessimistic way.

Accept that you have taken a side step off the path of your new way of being and decide to get back on it. Take a few good deep breaths and tell yourself you can do this. Then focus on the way you want to be and start again with positive thoughts.

Say to yourself something positive. Maybe 'calm down', 'relax', 'I can do this I know I can', 'I believe I am great', 'I am worthwhile and special'. Take another step towards your goal.

No, it's not easy; however, it is worthwhile and

when you realize that, once again, you have changed the attitude you have from negative to positive, and that yes, once again, you have picked yourself up, you will see that when you don't give in you will make it. When you reach this point, falling down, picking yourself up, you will achieve your dream.

No matter how many times you fall down you can pick yourself up. Never give up on yourself or your goal. Everything is within reach when you believe. It sounds so easy, doesn't it? All you have to do is believe in yourself, No matter how many times you let yourself know you do believe this, a horrible nagging doubt may pop up from within to tell you the opposite. It is this niggling doubt that causes the problem. This is the core belief you have in yourself. You can say to yourself you are confident, but when your core belief is not in alignment, things aren't going to change permanently.

There is work to do! You can do this. I know you can. I believe you can, and when you believe you can, you will. It's as simple as this, when you believe you can, totally and utterly believe, you will.

Why not spend time over the next few days thinking about yourself. Long, hard thoughts. What do you tell yourself? Is there anything positive in your mind about you? Maybe not. Negative thoughts are demotivating. They are lies that you constantly tell yourself. Why is this? It is so easy to believe the negative stuff about yourself, and when you focus on this it brings you down.

Are you putting on a brave face throughout your day? Do the people in your life, even your family, have no idea that you may be drowning inside? If you could trust someone and open up to them, you will start to recover. I know it will be difficult to do. You may have tied yourself in knots inside with the negative thoughts that you are having. When you realize that it is these negative thoughts—how you are thinking—that are the cause of your problem, then you can begin the change.

When you take the first tentative step and let yourself know, yes, you are worthwhile, you will begin to surface from the quagmire of your mind. Face the demons within your mind. Tell them that enough is enough: you are going to change, you are sick and tired of all the lies and negative information you have been channeling inside to yourself.

Let yourself know in no uncertain terms that today is the day. You are going to stand up and be counted, you are going to claim back yourself, your life, your happiness. You are entitled to happiness in your life, and when you go from negative thinking to positive you can change.

Only you can do this. You will have to reach down deep inside you and will it into being. Don't give in to the horrible things you tell yourself. Stay alert on your thoughts. It is vital that you bring optimism into your mind.

Make the intention daily when you wake up.'Today my thoughts are positive. I am happy and my day will be wonderful'. Make up your own words if those don't sit well with you, but please, make your first thoughts positive.

It sounds easy, doesn't it. But when you have

programmed negativity into your mind for years and years, it's not going to be easy to change. You can do it. I know you can. I want you to change. I want this because you want it and I want you to have a happy life. You are entitled to be a happy, confident person. You were not put on this Earth to be miserable, so please don't be miserable.

Get rid of negative thoughts and change them to ones that make you feel good inside. You can do this when you make the intention to change. Hold on to that intention through thick and thin. When you feel yourself slipping back into old habits, old negative thoughts, change them back instantly and smile to yourself. Let yourself feel good by saying something wonderful about you. You are wonderful. You are worthwhile. You do have a purpose. Once you accept that the cause of your problem is inside your mind, you will be able to change. An intent is powerful. Write down your intent. State it aloud to yourself whenever you can. Before thinking about what you want to do or what you want to have, ask yourself who you want to be. If, you feel like you have failed in your attempt at living the life you want, you can if you wish decide to be different. Be gentle. Be wise. Be willing to be kind to yourself. Get some index cards and write down your intent. Post them everywhere. Read them aloud, especially when you're tempted by old limited thinking. This works.

Monitor your thoughts. Pay attention to how often you move into worry, negativity, fear, anxiety, and for now, just gently notice it. Don't get upset when you forget. Stay alert, watch them, it is these thoughts that unconsciously send you out of your intent. Reaffirm your intent, and, if you are motivated enough you can add affirmations when you hear yourself worrying or saying things you aren't happy about.

You will eventually alter your ego and listen with your heart. At this time you will believe what you say, and you will know you have changed how you were into how you want to be.

It can also help to write your feelings down on paper. There is no need to let anyone know that you are doing this, and there's no need to keep what you write should you not want to. Destroy or burn those negative thoughts, release them from your mind by this action. Knowing what you are dealing with, in this case, your negative thoughts, is half the battle to improving your life.

You are not alone with this problem, although you may feel you are. People put on a brave face most of the time, but inside they may be nervous. They don't show it; and they take up the challenge to overcome those doubts and fears and move through them. This is what you should do. Move through them. Move past them. When you come to realize you have potential, that you aren't much different from other people throughout the world, you should, I hope, start to see the light at the end of the tunnel.

Bring hope and determination into your life. Stick with it no matter how long it takes; stay positive. Ditch the negativity, it's a weight that drags you down. It suffocates you and stops you from living your life the way you want. Your ego doesn't care that you are down, it knows no difference whether you are happy or sad. It accepts that this is what it is. This is how things will stay unless you bring hope and determination within you.

5

TAKE CONTROL

Did you realize that you create your own fear? You do this by thinking about negative outcomes to whatever it is that you want to do. If you can cause this feeling in yourself, it makes sense that you can also change it.

How can you do this? You first need to accept that you are imagining failure before you have even attempted what you hope to achieve It is these thoughts that cause you to be scared.

When you stop to think about this, surely, if these feelings are created by imagination, then if you replace the negative thoughts with thoughts of a successful outcome, this will help lower your stress.

For example, you may be scared of flying, because

you worry about the plane crashing on taking off or landing. If you can try and focus on something totally unrelated to the worries you have as the plane is leaving or landing, this will take away the nervousness you have, and help you stay calm and relaxed.

Remember, the way you think forms how you feel, so, you create your own fears. When you start to concentrate on things that might go wrong, or when you are fearful about something, replace your thoughts with a positive successful outcome.

Try thinking about a past event that you enjoyed to take your mind off your nervousness. Your self talk will play an important part in getting rid of your stress.

When you tell yourself bad things are going to happen, this increases your stress level, and makes you feel scared. Your sub-conscious mind accepts the information it has been told and goes into panic mode on your behalf!

So remember, let your subconscious hear strong

confident words, that will help keep it, and you, calm, and before you know it you will be able to do easily what in the past used to frighten you!

Life isn't easy. Ups and downs, curves and hills, but it is the one shot you have at making it how you want. You can do this, even though at this moment you may be feeling hopeless.

The trick is to let yourself know that no matter what happens you can and will get through the day. Keep this mindset as often as you can.

Don't concern yourself with tomorrow, take the positives from yesterday and grow within. Stay strong in the belief in yourself and know that each day you will be stronger than the one before.

It is not easy to be content with how you are when you aren't the way you want to be. You can choose how you want to be purely by changing the thoughts you have.

Unfortunately, not so easy to do. Maybe you need advice, maybe you need someone to talk to first to enable you to move through what it is that is holding you back, or making you feel unimportant and giving you misery.

Talk to your medical practitioner, go to an organization that can help you. Ask around. If you can pluck up the courage to do this, I say pluck up the courage because you may be living your life showing no one how you actually feel. You may be concealing everything inside, bottling it up to the extent that those people in your life don't realize for one second the turbulence that occurs inside your mind every day. Seek out the experts. Find a help line in your area who is prepared to listen. Sometimes, it's what you need to enable you to start those tentative steps toward your recovery.

As hard as it is, open up to an understanding person and let them know how you feel. Listen to what they say. Because you listen, it does not mean that you have to go with what they tell you. It is important, however, to pay attention and think hard about whether what they say will be of help to you, and will enable the person you are now to become the person you want to be.

You don't have to do anything that will not help you. Just because they have given their advice doesn't give them the right to force or entice you to become the way they suggest, or do what it is they have told you. Know you are in charge of your life. This life is your one shot at living, and so it has to be in the way that is right for you.

Everything in your life should be there because you want it to be. Move past anything that you did not invite or do not want. Attract what you want by being open and honest in the way you deal with the people you come into contact with throughout your day.

When you sit at home and mope, you are not helping yourself to change. Take the decision to do something with your life. I know it won't be easy, but you really should attempt to go places where you can meet people. You could take a night class. No matter how old you are, it is never too late to start something new. Go to art classes, take up photography, take sewing lessons, join the gym, do flower arranging, attend church services. Go to places where you can mingle and speak to people. If you are shy and withdrawn, this will not be easy, but if you sit where no one is, you aren't going to help yourself.

Be brave. Reach deep down within and say hello to someone. When you get that longed for reply, start asking the person questions. About what? About themselves, their hobbies, where they live, what movies they like, what food they enjoy. Ask them anything to give you both time to relax and become used to each other.

Should the person you speak to not be forthcoming, don't give up, move on to somebody else to talk to. Seek out the person who is on his own and chat. This person may be feeling the same way as you, wishing the ground would swallow him up because he knows no one. You never know you might be making a friend for life. Unless you give this a go, you will never know, will you?

6

ATTITUDE

I know what lies ahead of you will not be easy because when you may be at a low ebb, it is not easy to pull yourself back from these feelings. The fact that you are still reading this book must be of significance. I take it as a sign that you have turned a huge corner in your life and have taken the first tentative step along the road to better feelings, the road of searching for an answer on how to have a meaningful life, one in which you love and are loved because of who you are.

A big thing that you have to learn is how to love yourself. I know it won't be easy because you may have spent your life letting yourself know how useless you are, how ugly, how fat, how skinny, how much of a waste of space you have become. You are no waste of space. I am sure that within you is a spark of human decency that is longing to be brought to life, that longs to change. I believe you want to change how you are. I know it won't be easy. I also believe that with the right attitude, you will be able to help yourself. *With the right attitude*, is that all it will take? Well, maybe not, but it will be a start towards the new you. The thoughts you have, have made you who you are, and they have formed your life into what you have today, now, at this point in time.

How is your attitude? Do you wake up in the morning, and if it's sunny you feel good, and so you have a good day. If it's cold or raining, do you say what a lousy day it is, and this affects your attitude, and so your day is not as good as it was yesterday, when the sun was shining?

Have you had one of those days when nothing seems to go right? The alarm never went off, there's no milk left for your coffee. Is it at this point you say 'Nothings going to go right today'.

As if to prove you right, the car refuses to start, and when you eventually arrive late to work, your co-worker smiles at you but on seeing your mood, her smile fades, her good mood disappears within minutes.

You're so busy, no time for a lunch break, and then the computer crashes. How's your attitude at this point? How's that co-worker feeling? To cap it all off there's a traffic hold up on the way home.

When you eventually get home to your partner, do you say 'I told you it was going to be one of those days, and I was right'. A great percentage of how you feel on any one day is determined by the way you want to feel. What you expect most to happen, increases the chance of it happening.

If you think about attitude, it is contagious isn't it? It only takes one person to be in a bad mood, and this infects the next person who passes it on to the next one and so everyone ends up in a bad mood, and all because of that one person.

You can control your attitude, and let's face it, sometimes it's the only thing we can have control over. Most of us have so much to be thankful for. A roof over our heads three meals a day, people who love us, friends who care about us. Sometimes we tend to forget this don't we? The choice is yours whether you endure your life or enjoy it.

Personal responsibility plays a huge part here. It's no good blaming someone else for things that have gone wrong in your life as a result of the choices you made. You may have a problem agreeing with this, but you have to be responsible for some of what has gone wrong in your lifetime. Can you change? Yes, of course you can. No matter how old or how young you are, you can always change. Start right now, this minute if you want to. If you think this isn't possible, ask yourself why this is. It's a matter of changing the thoughts you have and making them your reality. Whatever your next thought is, it can change your life. Right now, this minute.

Understand that you hold the key to your future. This may sound daunting, and it may not be easy for you to better yourself. It all depends on how much you want this. Is it a top priority? If not, it may be because you don't believe you are special and an important human being.

Where did things go wrong? At what point in your life did things start to go downhill? Were you a small child who knew no better? As a child, you have to look to older people to help you. Perhaps you felt that no one cared about you? So many children feel this way. Each child, and this does include you, deserves to be loved. Each child is so very important, but sometimes the adult doesn't care, that love and hugs are not being given, and the child may become insecure and feel unwanted.

It may have been your start in life that has made you dislike yourself and what you are. However, all is not lost. You have survived so far, and what you should do is look within to become the new you. It's all there, locked away inside you. It may be a bit worse for wear, after all, you may have suffered for many years and felt unimportant for so long. However, what you have inside you doesn't die, doesn't give up, but lies waiting. It never gives up on you as a beautiful person it knows you to be.

If only you could see within you, see the beautiful you that is waiting to emerge. This, on its own, would bring you hope. At this point of time in your life, things may have gone wrong, and at the moment you may see no light at the end of the tunnel, and so may be filled with dread. The thought of bettering yourself may fill you with fear. Maybe you will get hurt, maybe you will not do well, maybe you will fail again, and when you do so, maybe you will fall back down and not know which way to turn. I shall tell you. The way to turn is within. Here lies the answer to your problems.

7

CREATE YOUR FUTURE

When you believe in yourself you will find there is so much more that you can achieve in your life.

Did you know that if you desire a life with peace of mind and harmony, it is a possibility? What you have to realize is that you hold the key to making this happen.

You have the ability to create your future. You might rely on other people in your life to fulfill your needs and wants, but you may never be entirely satisfied with what they provide, because you are the one who knows what's right for you.

If you want to live your life in a way that is filled with healthy relationships, a strong career, or whatever you desire, you will need to be totally honest with yourself and how you are.

Do you live your life in the way others expect of you, and not the way you wish to? Sometimes it becomes easier to be how others expect us to be than to step out of our comfort zone and change doesn't it?

It may be difficult for you initially, but if you really do want to help yourself, it will be of benefit to you to become attuned with your emotions. In this way you can be totally honest with what it is you want in your life, and how you intend to change it.

Acknowledge yourself, and realize your self worth. You may feel anger, or jealousy, fear, or other emotions, but you need to become comfortable with how you are. Yoga, meditation or writing a daily journal can help you become the person you truly want to be. Meditation is a wonderful way to relax your mind and body. There are many benefits you can gain by meditating on a daily basis. Whenever possible sit at the same time each day.

Meditating can often assist in reducing stress. It can also improve health and well-being. You may be surprised once you practice this regularly at just how good you will begin to feel. Your health should improve, and you should feel more relaxed and at peace within yourself. You will be able to cope better with normal everyday things that used to really bug you in the past! I am sure you will benefit in all the ways mentioned.

When you begin, allow your mind and body to relax as you let go of the pressures of the day. Sit with eyes closed, or open. Take some slow deep breaths and allow yourself to just 'be in the moment'. Don't try to stop your thoughts flowing and try not to dwell on anything that comes into your mind.

Just let the thoughts come and go, you may see faces floating in front of you. You may have unusual thoughts. Don't be alarmed, accept everything that flows in through your mind.

Stay relaxed this way until you are ready to return to normality. Take a couple of minutes to come to normal wakefulness. You should feel calm and relaxed and ready to face the rest of your day with renewed energy!

When you do this regularly you will benefit by increased energy. The renewed vitality and confidence you will gain will make you feel fantastic!

Meditation restores the body's state of balance. When you are in a state of balance you are more able to heal yourself due to the feelings of well-being you have.

You will also gain a greater sense of self-awareness. The more you do it the more aware you will become of your own capabilities. As you become attuned to this energy you will find yourself becoming more aware of your potential as a human being. You will become intuitive and discover the amazing potential you have had all along that has been lying dormant within you. You will be more accepting of people around you, whereas in the past you may have you been short tempered, or not inclined to understand others. You will be surprised at how confident you will feel and the inner strength you have gained.

The new person you have become will give you the foundation for a truly wonderful future. A future the way you want it to be.

8

SELF LOVE

Loving yourself is vital to your improvement, and everything hinges on you being able to say 'I love myself'.

Many find it difficult, if not impossible to say. However, with determination, it is possible. Why not give it a go now? Close your eyes and say 'I love myself'. Let the words wash over you as you say them. Think about what you have said. Wonderful feelings when you say it often enough. I want you to say this as often as you can. Any time that you think you can't cope, say 'I love myself'; get used to the words, you need them in your life.

You have to love yourself, and when you do, you will start to heal. The healing starts with self-love because then you will begin to understand that, yes, there is a light at the end of the tunnel. You will realize that, yes, I am loveable, and yes, I am going to get through this. Why? Because you love yourself.

Now comes the hard part, or maybe not. When you love yourself, how can you fail? I know, not true, you may fail, but because you have love in your heart, you will know that what you are trying to do makes you special, and when you attempt to do something and fail, it doesn't matter, because you have self-love, self-worth, and you know that you will eventually achieve. It is what you are meant to do.

Why would you want to suffer any longer now you have discovered it is within your power to become a capable, wonderful human being. Your past thoughts may have lead you astray, it has happened to many of us. It's how you get yourself back on the path that is important. Some take years to get back on to the path and some unfortunately never do. I know that because you are still listening to me, you are not going to fail. I hope you are going to do your best and that no matter how long it takes, you are able to improve your life because you deserve a better one.

How to do this? You should give up bad habits. You have to learn that when you do wrong, you pay the consequence. If you are putting dependency drugs into your body, you aren't going to help yourself because you will always be dependent on the drugs; you have to be dependent on yourself. Is this what scares you? Being dependent on yourself? You can do this. Once you unlock the inner you, you will have the wisdom to know what you are doing wrong, and have the desire to set things right in your life.

The scary thing is that only you can do it. Perhaps that's not what you hoped to hear, but how can you improve yourself when you don't make the effort. Remember, you have the inner you to fall back on, and this inner you loves you totally. Listen to the thoughts you have. It is these thoughts that are either helping you or making you unhappy.

I have mentioned how important your thoughts are. Pay attention to them, choose the ones that are helpful to you, and not the ones that you have had in the past. You don't need ones where you put yourself down, where you tell yourself you can't do things.

Maybe you have always told yourself you are useless, and no one in their right mind will ever love you because you don't deserve love. What makes you think you don't deserve love? Each of us deserve love. Love is the most important thing in our lives. It is important to have love in your life. If at the moment, you may feel no one loves you, put that thought to the back of your mind and tell yourself how much you love the person you are and the person you plan to become in the future.

You see, the problem is the thoughts you have are making you the way you are. When you spend your time choosing thoughts that make you unhappy, this is how you are. Did you know that your subconscious doesn't know the difference between a lie and the truth? It's true, and so you know what this means? Each time you have said something about yourself that was not very nice, your subconscious has picked up this information and believed it because it knows no difference. Why would it, you are in charge of your thoughts, aren't you? Why choose thoughts that make you unhappy, that keep you tied down and bogged under in misery, when you can choose thoughts that at least bring you hope.

Start to watch carefully the thoughts that come into your mind It may not be easy at first because of the long time you may have dwelt on the negative things about yourself.

The more you focus on the unhappiness in your life, the worse your life becomes. Each time you drag to the front of your mind something that annoys you or makes you angry, you re-ignite the flame and make things worse. Try to stop doing this. It has to be better to focus on things that make you strong and confident rather than things that make you sad and unsure of yourself. Do you feel that nothing makes you happy? I believe we all have at least one thing that brings us happiness?

Do you have a family who care about you, even though you may believe they don't? Why do you think this is so? Is your self esteem so low that you feel nobody likes you or wants to be with you. As often as you can change your negative thoughts into 'I am a positive person and people like to be around me'. You may not believe this at the moment, but when you say these things to yourself often enough, it will become true to you.

Do you remember what was said about your subconscious not being able to tell the difference between a lie and the truth? Why not start today by telling it that you are a wonderful human being? Say the words often until they become your reality.

9

PERSONAL RESPONSIBILITY

Do you sometimes think nothing is your fault, that everyone else is to blame? Life is about choices and you are what you have chosen to be. It's not always correct to say someone else is at fault for what has gone wrong in your life. It is the choices we make that form the reality that is now our life. Why not take time to sit back and have a think about what has been said. It's important and it's meant to help you.

Perhaps at the moment you are unhappy. I can only say to you that I hope some of what you read makes sense. However, it is up to you whether you accept what you have read and put steps in place to help you to change.

It's not a easy to accept that perhaps you are responsible for how you are. Should you be blaming someone else, what did they do or say to make you how you are? When they said or did something that you weren't happy with, or disagreed with, how did you react? Did you shout, and argue with them? If so, what happened next? Did you accept what they said and allow it to seep into your mind and heart and make you the way you are. As hard as this is to discover, you chose to accept what was said and you then went with it. I know you are probably thinking that you had no option. However, the fact that you felt you had no option must show that you had a choice and you chose to accept what was said even though it made you unhappy.

Why did this happen? It may have been as a result of your conditioning in the past. I go back to your childhood again where so much pain sometimes start. This may be because you were so impressionable as a child, as are we all, but it is sad to say that many adults are not cautious with what they say to children. They are unaware when something they have said has upset the child. Children also can be cruel and say things to each other that can cause huge problems throughout life.

I can speak from personal experience on this. When I was about five or six years of age, I walked up to join with two children who were playing together. One of them looked up at me and told me to go away as they didn't want to play with me. I went away feeling very upset at the rejection.

However I didn't realize at that time how those words would affect me throughout my life. I was far too young to understand anything other than feeling upset. The hurt feeling was my reaction to the words.

I spent my life standing aside not joining in because I felt I wouldn't be wanted. I also lacked confidence, and basically felt pretty miserable because of not feeling important. This didn't cease as I grew into adulthood, it remained with me and still does to a certain extent. I have to work hard at pushing myself forward knowing I am a result of words spoken to me.

Now that I am older I am aware that had I

thought nothing of what was said to me and went off to play elsewhere, I wouldn't have had the problems I had as I grew up. I know it's not easy to change. I know watching what you think and how you react is not easy, but when you become aware that it is your own thought and reaction that either help or hinder you, you will be able to improve over time.

Was this you? I know it happens to children in all walks of life, be they rich or poor, educated or not. We are all a result of what we have been taught, or told whilst growing up.

Some children go through life without affection and this tends to close them off to giving affection in later life. Others may have had no love shown, but they have become strong within as they grew and they become determined that when they have children those children will know the pleasure and the amazing love that can be passed on through a hug. It's so important to love and be loved.

This is where problems often arise. Do you love yourself? What did you reply, was it a firm no. Do you think you are worthless? Why do you think this when you yearn to be loved, or long to have someone in your life who finds you worthy and not lacking.

You may be the result of people telling you their negative thoughts on how they think you are. When this happens don't pay attention to what has been said, dismiss what you have heard. They were that person's thoughts not yours. When you can do this you will save yourself pain and stop those low feelings and miserable thoughts that come later on as you think about what was said. Of course this is easy to say, difficult, in fact sometimes very difficult to do, and it's only when you come to realize that, in fact, your thoughts do make your reality that you come to understand this.

10

INNER CHANGE

Can you see then that when you change the thoughts you have, you will be able to change how you feel on the inside? No, it's not easy, but then nothing worth achieving is going to be easy, is it?

It will be trial and error, desperation at times, thoughts of giving up, thoughts of 'is it worth it', 'why do I bother'. Why do you bother? I hope it's because you want more in your life, far, far more than you have at the moment.

The change must come from within. No one can give you this inner growth. People can give you advice. A life coach may well be able to offer very good help that can assist you along your pathway to discovering a new you, but when push comes to shove, it is you, yes *you*, who is the only one who can change. The change has to come from within because this is where your problem lies. It's not the struggle to find a job, to find the perfect partner, to find someone who treats you kindly, to give you things that you need. It's within you that has to change, and once you understand this and put the thoughts in your head in a pattern that helps you to become the way you want, you are going to ease your problem, and start to change.

You may have glimpses of euphoria when you believe you are happy, but this may soon disintegrate when the happiness wasn't coming from a place deep within you but came as a result of something outer that may have brought a glimpse of happiness. Maybe someone gave you a gift or said something nice about you, or paid you a compliment. Did this feel good? Of course it did, and as a result, you may have savored this compliment, brought it back into your mind and felt the happiness, the sheer pleasure it brought. Why did it bring you pleasure again and again? Because you kept thinking about it, and it was this thought that brought you happiness.

Can you see then, that when someone says something negative to you, and you take it to heart and keep thinking about it, you are reinforcing the hurt that the words gave you and each time you are reliving the pain. Yet again, it is your thoughts that are making your reality.

The difficult part is not reacting to the words that hurt. I know, it's so easy to say isn't it, but not always easy to do. However, when you can put those words out of your mind you will lessen the pain.

Be strong and when someone says something that hurts you and say something positive to yourself. Perhaps, 'I am not like that. I am a worthwhile person', or some other personal words that rest easy with you that you find helpful to enable you to stay strong.

The more determined you are to stay positive, the more you will come to appreciate that you are actually changing. Slow and sure wins the race. Don't get frustrated when you feel you are slipping back into old habits. It will take time to change, but unless you at least keep trying, things will stay the same.

So what do you think? Do you feel you would like to give change a go? Only you can decide and only you can do this. It's going to be difficult. I can only say to you: don't give up whatever you do.

I am sure that inside you is this wonderful spirit that is waiting to be set free, and once you do this, you will find there is nothing you won't be scared to try.

Have you had things in mind that you would so love to do. Maybe you told someone who laughed at the thought of you doing this. Did they say you were too old or not clever enough or wasting your time, or did they just roll their eyes at you and walk away.

Whatever they said, did you take it to heart and go with their idea of you? Did you feel that had you given it a go, you would have been successful? If so, it was at this point you could have dismissed the negative reaction the person gave you, and put positive thoughts into place to let yourself know that no matter what had been said, you were going to do it. When you look back, do you regret not trying? It's never too late. It all depends on you, whether you are prepared to swallow your fear and decide to at least attempt to do it. Fearful thoughts will hold you back. To get rid of fear you have to stop feeding your mind negative information.

It's these thoughts that bring anxiety, and then, because you accept them into your mind, you instantly limit your ability. When you dismiss the thought, refuse to accept it, you will feel better within yourself.

When you think you can't do something then this is what happens. When you trust yourself and believe you can, you will improve your confidence, because the more often you talk in a confident way the stronger you will feel.

You have the ability to alter the way you are. Once you believe this, you can use your thoughts to change. The more you tell yourself about how capable you are, the sooner you'll become this way.

Strong confident self talk is essential. When you hear your thoughts becoming anxious, try to replace them with positive information. Don't let them take hold in your mind. You can choose to change your thoughts into something you want to hear.

When you feel scared do your best to ignore the thoughts, and change them into positive words. Tell yourself words such as 'I am not afraid', or, 'I am a brave confident person,' anything that will take your mind away from what scares you.

Why not attempt something that in the past you wouldn't have tried because you thought you would fail. Tell yourself that you can and will do it this time, and then stay determined, and try until you succeed.

Stay as confident as you can throughout your day. Replace any anxious thoughts that creep inside your mind with positive information, and don't listen to anyone who tells you negative things about yourself.

11

SUCCESS IN FAILURE

There is success in failing. You may feel upset when you fail at something, but you should take to heart the fact that you tried. This is where success lies. Failure would be in the fact that you never tried. Always attempt to do what your heart wants to. In this way, you will succeed even though you may not get it right.

When you attempt to do something, you will feel good. However, if you didn't succeed, have another go, and then another if need be. Each time you are unsuccessful, let yourself know what a good effort you just made, then try again. Visualize yourself as having succeeded, feel the confidence grow as you tell yourself you can, and will, do it. You will be successful providing you don't give up. People who give up have regrets, but when you finally succeed, you will be ready for the next challenge.

Challenge is good. In fact when you challenge yourself to do something, you can achieve. Stay determined and strong inside. You have an amazing spirit within. Put it to the test any time you want. It's always within you and prepared to help you to overcome.

You have to be aware of your ability, of your greatness. Yes, of your greatness. Never doubt yourself. I know, easy to say, but when you have the right 'can do' mindset, you will become stronger and will grow in confidence daily.

Everything you need is within you. Use it, trust it, test it, and learn your capabilities. No matter what you have been told in the past, you do have a great ability. It may be lying dormant within you at the moment because of your negative way of thinking, but it is there and can be molded and shaped into how you want to be, purely by changing your thought pattern.

You believe what you think. You become what

you believe. When the thoughts you have are lowering your confidence or telling you unpleasant things about yourself, they are your thoughts, your own beliefs, that make you who you are.

Change your mindset. Start talking to yourself in a positive way. Tell yourself anything you like provided it's positive information. It's easy to bring up unhappy events and rethink things that made us miserable in the past. How many times do you hash over arguments that happened a long time ago? Let the hurt and anger go. Nothing is gained by dragging up hurtful memories from the past. It's strange how often we do it though, isn't it? Time and time again we focus on what made us miserable. Each time we do it we bring up the hurt and anger. We may rehash words that were spoken. This time we say what we wished we had thought to say at the time. We normally come out on top when we look back, but this does nothing to stop the hurt feelings surfacing again. It serves no purpose looking back over old hurts from the past. If we were to think about happy times, we would feel more positive and much happier in our lives.

Make the effort to put past hurts behind you, and from today focus only on the happiness and occasions that have made you smile. Only when you let go of past hurts can you move forward with confidence.

You may feel stuck where you are and scared about moving forward, but when you reach within and trust your inner guidance, you will discover that you have a strength you only ever dreamed of. Still having doubts?

Have people told you they don't think you can do something when you have asked for their advice? The person you asked may have tried to help you in a way to suit themselves and not you. They may fear you may hurt yourself or do a better job than they could, or perhaps they feel they might lose you. Whatever their reason, it is you who stopped yourself, not them. It's easy to give in or throw in the towel even when you want to do something. Sometimes, it may be your own mind that is stopping you.

Perhaps you were given encouragement from the person you asked but lacked the faith in yourself to continue. You listened to that little voice within that told you there's no way you would be successful. This is your subconscious having a little chat with you and trying to keep you safe! It's agreeing with the fact that you dare not do something because it knows you. It is the sum total of all the information you have fed into your mind your whole life. When you are scared, it accepts this because you normally have these thoughts. It doesn't say let's give it a go, shall we? Or if it does, it quickly reverts to what it knows about you.

Remember, the subconscious cannot tell the difference between the truth and a lie, and so you should change what you tell it straight away, even though at that moment you don't think much of your ability. You can change the way your subconscious sees you by instantly changing the thoughts to positive ones.

The more you confirm how special, important, capable, and worthwhile you are, the sooner your subconscious will come to believe it. Don't give up talking to it! Feed it all the positive information about yourself you can think of. However you want to be, tell your subconscious you are that way now. Self-talk is so important to making you the way you want to be, to changing your life.

You may not believe me at this point, but I truly hope you are prepared to at least try to change those thoughts from negative to positive. It is only through repetition, repeating the positive stuff every day as often as you can, that you will slowly notice the change.

A good idea is to write those positive things down every day. Why not buy a diary and write four affirmations each morning, and the same again each night before you go to sleep? Don't give up on this idea as being stupid because it does work. I know, it is something I do, and I feel it's very helpful and it reaffirms to me who I am.

How long can you go without saying something negative about yourself, either out loud or to yourself? Pay attention to the thoughts you have, you might find yourself having nothing but negative ones about yourself. When you do, instantly replace them with positive stuff. The root cause of your problem is your thought pattern.

When you believe in yourself, you will become a stronger, more confident person. You will radiate a whole new you to those who know you. You will find you will attract different people, people who will be impressed by your confident attitude and who will want to be with you because of how positive you are. People like being around positive people. Positive people make others feel positive!

You may find that many of the people around you at the moment are negative. There is no doubt about it because negative attracts negative, like attracts like, and so it is up to you. Are you happy in the company of negative thinkers? This surely isn't what you want for your life. Change those thoughts to positive and attract positive people!

12

STAY DETERMINED

Are you fed up reading self-help books, and watching those self-help movies? Is nothing helping? Have you thought that maybe they aren't helping because you have found it difficult to act on what they say? You may have read books and watched movies but nothing worked. What happened when nothing worked for you? Did you give up in frustration? Not giving up is the key to success. Don't give up on yourself. Don't give in to frustration. Each time you do, you fall back down in your confidence. Each time you fall back, you go lower and lower in your disbelief. You must fight for what you want, and when what you want is to be strong and confident, to love and be loved, change how you are by changing what you think about yourself.

You will not be confident when you think you can't do something and keep telling yourself this. You will not believe in yourself when you insist on telling yourself that you are not worthwhile, that everyone is better than you. I tell you no one is better than you. It doesn't matter that someone has a big house, a new car, lots of money. You could have all this and still not be happy when you don't think much of yourself.

So what to do? Become determined to change and stay determined. No matter how low you go you will continue to dislike yourself when you feel you are getting nowhere. Stay above the frustration and work your way back by refusing to give up. Don't sink into despair. Know that you are a worthwhile human being and that you are responsible for yourself. You hold the key to your betterment. The key is within you. Stop looking around you for the answer because it isn't there. No matter how far and wide you search, it's not there.

You may have things happen externally that bring you happiness, but in the long scheme of things, this happiness is fleeting and will go because of how you feel and how you believe yourself to be.

You might be in total disagreement with what is being said. I understand this, because until you accept responsibility for how you are, you may not accept that what you are thinking is the cause of how you are. You may still be blaming others for the way your life has turned out. Its difficult to accept that you might have done things wrong when you find yourself in a place you don't want to be. Not until you understand that the cure is within will you heal. You are the result of your thought talk. Everything in your life is the result of your thoughts. When you aren't happy, it's because you are thinking unhappy thoughts. When you are happy, it's because you are having happy thoughts.

When you change the sad thoughts, you help yourself become happy. Slowly but surely you will improve how you are. Only you can do this. It doesn't matter how many times your hear this, unless you act on it, things will remain as they always have, and you may spend your time wondering why nothing goes right for you. You may see yourself as not having any friends and believe everyone seems so much happier and have more than you. They probably don't, but because you are unhappy and dissatisfied, you believe they have.

People have problems but they deal with them in different ways. Some people look at their problems as challenges, they embrace them head on and actually enjoy them. I know, that doesn't seem quite right, does it? These people are the fighters, they refuse to give up on themselves, and they work on how they are. They don't give in and moan and groan about their lives, they knuckle down, get stuck in, embrace the challenge, look it straight in the eyes and then make the changes and work their way through each thing that has to be done.

They may not get the result they hoped for, but this doesn't deter them. They look back and see where they went wrong, and either redo what they failed at or learn from the mistake, don't worry and fret about it, but accept that this was what happened, get over it, and move on with their lives.

This is what I am hoping you can do. Put things behind you. Decide today that you have a clean slate in front of you. A whole new you waiting to move forward. Slowly but surely, work your way through any challenges you may come up against. Don't think you can't cope, this is not the talk that helps. Let yourself know that you are going to do your best to get through. Then do whatever you have to do. When you achieve what you set out to do, stop and congratulate yourself. It doesn't matter how small the challenge was, or how big, the fact that you tried makes you an achiever. Feel thankful and strong that you have moved forward, be it a tiny step or a huge stride.

The fact that you did something positive should make you feel confident and better able to cope the next time. I know this is a lot to take in, and it's easy for me to say to you to do this or do that, but it is you that holds the key to your future. Nobody else does, you do. Can you understand and accept this? You may have been blaming others for years, and you might find it hard to accept that the fault lies at your feet and not with someone else. You have choices, and the choices you have made in the past result in how you are today.

13

CHOICES

Throughout your life people will hurt you. Often, not because they set out to hurt you, but because they may have been upset or feeling low themselves and they may have spoken hastily and harshly without thinking about the consequences.

Unfortunately, you may not have not dismissed their words, but have locked into them, taken them to heart, and lived with them burning away inside. Some words hurt. Some words are given with the best intentions in the world as advice in the hope of helping, but it is how they are received that is the vital thing.

When words are perceived as being hurtful, as not being true, or just not what were wanted at the time, the reaction is so important and how you receive them is the answer to having a problem later, or not having a problem at all. Don't let the words into your heart. dismiss them from your mind, refuse to think of them, and think instead of something that makes you happy, gives you pleasure, no matter how small. Perhaps the sun is shining, or maybe something happened earlier that brought a smile to you. Anything, no matter what, grab on to it, think about it, again and again, because it made you happy, and in this way you can stop focusing on the hurtful words that you do not want in your mind or in your life.

When you discipline your mind, you allow yourself to achieve much more than you think you are capable of. If there is something you really want to achieve, you have to be willing to take a chance, even though you may be afraid. If you don't take the risk, the opportunity may be gone for ever.

Much depends on how you see yourself. What type of person do you feel you are? Are you capable, or do you believe that you normally don't do a very good job? Whatever your answer is, it is these thoughts that make you the way you are. You know what this means don't you? It is possible change the way you are if you want to.

Of course, it's not quite that easy. However, if you are determined, and can discipline your mind, it is possible. The first thing you have to do is believe that you can change.

When your doubts have been caused by other people's comments, it is important that you stop listening to this negative information. You have to retrain your subconscious mind to accept that you are an amazing human being! What a great thought, and you can be this, if you truly believe in yourself. Start by listening to how you think of yourself. Do your own thoughts put you down? Are you saying you can't rather than you can? It's those negative thoughts that are causing your problem. I know that sounds too easy, but it is true. You are the result of how you see yourself. Why not start by seeing yourself in a positive way?

A negative reaction can affect your life for years. I know this, because as I have said earlier in this book, my negative reaction to what was said to me as a child, who knew no better, has lasted throughout my life. It's only with determination that I have overcome this problem. Although being honest, I still suffer at times from feelings of unimportance. Some words sear deep and I think the fact I was so young has caused much of the problem I have.

I often wonder how my life would have turned out had I not cared about those damaging words that were spoken all those years ago.

You can choose what you want in your life. You can. I know this may be difficult to accept or maybe you do accept but it is putting it into practice that you find difficult. Remember though, the answer is always within.

Everything you need is within you, and when the time comes that you can search within, dig deep down inside and find that brave being, this is when you will begin to live the life you yearn.

The fact that you are reading this book shows that

you are not happy with your life the way it is at the moment. Do you look at others and wish you were living the same life they were. Do you think everything was easy for them because they are happy? Are they happy? Do you know this for certain, or do you assume this is so because of how they are behaving.

Many people can put on a good act, and although they may appear to be happy they have problems. Maybe not the same sort of problems that you have, but problems to them that make them unhappy, but they stay on top of them because they choose to.

My hope for you is that you choose to stay on top of your problems. Maybe we should stop calling them problems and refer to them as challenges. Challenge implies that with the right will and effort you will be able to get through.

Nobody is saying it is going to be easy. It's going to be far more worthwhile when you get to the other side. However, you may get to the other side of the challenge and find that the outcome is not at all as you expected. Sometimes things will have changed for the better or sometimes for the worse.

What you have to do is to remain objective and look back at what has happened to you. Dissect it, and see where things happened, how you coped, or maybe didn't cope. Look for the positives where you feel you could have done better, and look for where you can see you went wrong. It's now important for you to put behind what you did wrong and learn from it, decide not to do it again. Take the positive stuff with you, take the good things within you, and seep the good feeling within you where you feel you did well.

How wonderful, when you do something well, won't that be good to know? You achieved at something! When this has happened, give yourself a pat on the back and move forward along your life path.

14

POSITIVE THOUGHT PATTERN

Do you have moments of joy or moments of happiness? Are they fleeting, no sooner come than gone? When they are there, you have awoken the spirit within you. We all have one; each and every person on this Earth has an inner spirit. It is when you are developing, and trust this spirit, that you are able to cope with things in an easier way.

Have you heard people say that they go with their gut? This is when they have reached inside to that place where they are given information, sometimes information that they don't know the answer to but it came with a feeling or hunch, and when they have gone with this reaction they discover that their thoughts were right.

This is what you should do. Go with the gut as

often as you can. You will find the more you trust what the inner you tells you the more you are right. Sometimes you may think or hear thoughts that make you uneasy or scared of doing, but please take courage and go with what it is that you hear. Of course if for some unknown reason, your thoughts are to hurt someone, or do something bad then you aren't connecting with your inner spirit; you may be connecting with your ego that knows all about jealousies and wanting revenge. The inner you is goodness. It is connected to the heart center and the heart doesn't want to make you unhappy or give you horrible impulses to hurt others. Listen to the heart for it will speak truth to you.

When you go with what you hear or feel you will begin to go from strength to strength as you realize what you are hearing is bringing confidence. The more confidence you gain in yourself, the more you will be able to cope with everyday living.

You have to go within to find the answers you seek. You have much knowledge within, all there waiting to be tapped into to enable you to move your life in the direction you wish. Your inner voice is mighty. It will advise you on what to do, it may suggest study time, learning, but these things may take you out of your comfort zone and unless you are prepared to trust this inner voice you will not have the life you yearn for.

What you have to remember is that not everyone is confident one hundred percent of the time. Some people are able to show an outer layer of confidence when if truth be known they are shaking inside. You should aim for putting on a confident face, one that lets people think you are able to cope when maybe only you know the truth.

Having said this if you are suffering from an illness or depression that is getting you down do seek professional advice, because it is only when you have spoken to someone who understands, that you will be able to at least attempt to improve how you feel. Always remember, you are never alone. No matter how you feel, how sad, how helpless, there is always someone there who is prepared to listen.

If you don't believe this to be true, then you are the one who makes it so. It is this belief that will hold you back, and so you are urged to seek help, reach out to someone you trust. They may be able to assist with who can give you help. Maybe you just need someone to open up to and when you speak to a person who gets you, who understands what you are going through it is from this moment you should be able to move forward. Take a small step towards inner belief.

Should you feel you have no one who understands, there are groups, such as the Salvation Army, the Church, Samaritans, local advice bureau, counselor, or a medical practitioner who will be able to offer you help. Don't sit back and say there is no one who can help. Reach out.

This is the first step in your recovery. The first step in building your life in the way that is right for you. It is only when you have the belief in yourself that things will change, and you change how you are by the way that you think of yourself.

You want to have a positive, happy life, and yet

this will pass you by when you don't have enough confidence to do what you want. You are entitled to what is right for you. It is through the choices you make that you grow within.

When you think you sometimes had no choice to do other than what you didn't want, the fact that you decided not to do it was also a choice. Perhaps you took this decision because of not wanting to hurt someone's feelings. Maybe they told you they felt you weren't able, perhaps they said it for what they felt was the right reason, perhaps your safety? Whatever the reason you still made the choice to agree with what they said. This may be difficult to accept but it is the truth. When you can accept this there will be hope, and when there is hope this is a huge positive toward your change.

Whether it's a yes or a no, you do have a choice. Your choice will always have a consequence, and so you need to choose carefully. Choose what makes you feel good, what makes you happy, and, above all, what you want to do.

This is the way to go. Live your life in the way that suits you. Not everyone will agree with what you choose, but that doesn't mean you made the wrong choice. Go with your gut feeling, your intuition, your heart, and you will know it was the right choice for you.

I know how easy it is for me to say this to you. I feel you may want to take the advice, but I have said that you have to go with your gut. What does your gut tell you to do? Does it want this desperately? In your heart, do you want to change how you are?

I know it's going to be difficult. Nothing worth achieving is going to be easy. I hope you may now be feeling determined and saying to yourself that you are going to do this. You may feel buoyed by the thought that you can change. You will be excited inside at the thoughts you are having and prepared at this time to do your best to change. Confidence is good! Confidence is sometimes fleeting because we allow our mind, or the subconscious to interfere, to tell us that we can't do something when we have got excited and stirred up inside at the thought of bettering ourselves.

Is this you at the moment? Are you longing to give things a go, telling yourself you are worthy and that you can do this? Are you listening to that voice inside your head that's telling you differently? It's so easy to give in to that voice isn't it? You may never have tried to do something because of this voice.

I ask you to change your thought pattern into a positive one. It is through letting your inner self know that you believe in yourself that you will begin to take those first tentative steps toward changing your thought pattern. When you want to change how you are this is a must.

15

MOTIVATION

When you are looking to improve the way you feel about yourself, what your thoughts tell you is how you will be. Always remember, your thoughts make your reality.

Decide in what way you want your life to change. What is it you want to improve, what are the things you aren't happy with?

There are ways to help improve your life, give you the self-confidence you may lack, and enable you to become how you want to be. Don't worry about things that you have no control over. When you hope to improve your life because you are unhappy, this is something you are able to control.

So how do you want your life to be? Remember

it's your life, and your decision, so you need to make sure it will be the way you want.

Realize how special you are, and that you do have potential. Let yourself know that you deserve to have the very best that life has to offer. You have to believe this so that you can live your life to the fullest. Make sure that you allow your thoughts to know what you need to enable you to have what you want in your life.

Don't listen to comments from friends or family who may not agree with what you want to do. Stay in control of your life.

You are the result of your own thoughts. When you feel fed up and can't be bothered the result is that things won't get done. Have you started something with great enthusiasm only to find that you can't be bothered to make the effort? Why do you think this happens? What is happening is the result of your thought pattern. So what can you do?

Unless you motivate yourself nothing will change. What is happening in your life will continue until you work on your thoughts. Don't wish and wait for something to happen. Make the effort to do things. You do this by changing your thoughts.

Walk the dog, visit a friend, anything that activates you will help you feel good about yourself. When you are in that 'I can't be bothered' mood, try your best to get activated. You know how exciting and enjoyable it is to do something that you love. Try to apply this feeling and energy to lift and help motivate you. It's all too easy to tell yourself you can't be bothered. You miss out on much in your life when you feel this way.

Change those 'can't be bothered' thoughts into 'I am going to do this, because I know I can'. Keep on believing in yourself and strive ahead. Never accept 'I can't be bothered'. Become a stronger person by positive self talk. When you think positive thoughts about yourself, and about a successful outcome, you will succeed. You will be amazed at how different you feel within yourself when you have stuck at something and completed it to your satisfaction.

Don't look back with regret in a few years time at things you could have done, and should have done.

Stop hesitating - give it your best shot and have fun! When there's something you want to do, make the effort and do it! The rewards will be great when you do.

You may have set goals for yourself in the past and given up before you completed them. Deciding what you would like to do is the easy part, it's seeing it through to the end that causes the problem isn't it!

Do you have something that you really want to work on through to the end? If the answer is 'yes', start to put the wheels in motion for a successful result!

How do you do this? First you have to start to believe in yourself. Believe that you can achieve anything you wish! Choose the goal that is the most important to you and work on this one first.

Try visualizing a successful outcome to what you plan. Imagine people walking up to you shaking your hand, congratulating you on your success. Remember how this feels to you. It feels good, right? See this scene as often as you can.

Visualization is very powerful and it will work if you do it often enough. If you have a positive frame of mind you expect things to work for you, and more than likely they will, because what your mind expects it will get!

Stay positive on the outcome of the goal you want to achieve. Have you set a big goal? Split it up into smaller attainable goals. Finish each small goal before going on to the next. This will make things easier for you to deal with.

Read as much as you can about the subject you are interested in. Learn everything you can about it. Become knowledgeable. Is there someone who is successful in what it is that you plan? Can you talk to him/her? If so ask what was done to help him/her to achieve success. It really is a good idea to speak to the experts who have accomplished what you hope to.

An interesting way of goal setting is to first start by writing down the story of your life to date. Well, perhaps not everything! Write down the important experiences. Try to remember the turning points in your life, what successes you have had, what dreams. In fact write down what means the most to you.

If you can, narrow down your list to your greatest achievements, what disappointed you most, and what you feel were important lessons to you. This is a way to work out what is really important to you, your core values. When you have completed this list, the next thing to do is to write down what it is that you hope to achieve in the next five years.

This list is your road map, read it as often as you can. Particularly every morning and night. Do you dream of an overseas holiday? Do you want to take up studies to improve yourself, to change your job? What is it that you dream about?

You have to stay determined and focus on what you have to do to feed this vision. Keep the vision in your mind, hold it and work slowly and steadily towards it.

Visualizing a successful outcome plays a major part in this goal setting strategy. Visualizing your affirmations can help to make them a reality. Imagine what it is that you want to create in your life, then see yourself stepping into the picture in your mind.

See things vividly. What is it you want? If you long for a new car see yourself walking round it, look at the color, imagine how it will feel owning it. See yourself opening the door and getting inside. This car is something you really want, so imagine how you feel as you sit in it. Take a look around it, what can you see? What color seats have you chosen? What's on the dashboard?

See yourself turn the key, hear that motor start. Sounds good? Feels good? Watch the road as you drive away. Imagine how you are feeling as the car joins the traffic, or are you on a deserted road that leads to a place only you know of?

Describe to yourself what you are experiencing and how you feel. Don't watch the car drive away from you, make sure you are in it! What do you see as you drive along? What sounds can you hear? Make the experience as real as you can.

Write down your thoughts and the way you feel. Read these thoughts as often as you can and bring back the way you were feeling. Concentrate on these feelings, they are powerful, and will help you achieve your dream.

Cut out a picture of your dream car and pin it where you can see it. Recall how determined you are to own this car when you look at the picture.

Whatever it is that you want, step into the picture in your mind and affirm it until it becomes a reality. This is an amazing way to help yourself.

With a positive attitude and the right frame of mind there is no reason why you cannot achieve your dream.

16

YOU HOLD THE POWER

You are amazing. I repeat, you are amazing. When you don't believe this you won't be. Do you want to be? If you do, you have to work on how you speak to yourself. As I have said, you hold the power. The power is within. You are the power. When you accept this and decide you are going to change, you will feel a glimmer of hope; it will start from within and flare up inside you.

Keep the flare going by fueling the fire within with thoughts of how great you will be when you fully believe in yourself. You can do this. The answer is within your mind, it is your mindset. Change this mindset and grow into the person you long to be.

I hope by now you are feeling excited. I hope you

are coming to terms with the fact that you can, if you choose, change how you are.

Can you feel the wonderment rising within as you come to realize that you can change from now on? Perhaps not an instant change in how you are. Let's face it, good things take time and have to be worked on. Surely though you realize that once you change how you think, you will start to alter and can become how you want to be.

What is your biggest problem? Do you feel unworthy? Why should you? Do you believe others see you as being unworthy? If you were to tell them your feelings, I would like to bet they will be shocked that you believe this of them.

What I am saying is, what you are saying is just that, what you believe. What you believe has become your reality. You can change this belief to one that lets you know you are a worthwhile person. You are in control of your thoughts. Think about this for a moment. You are in control of your thoughts. They are in your mind only. No one knows your thoughts,

Thought Talk

only you, and when you don't like the thoughts you have about yourself, change them. Forget the negative stuff you have been listening to and change your thoughts into however you would like to be.

To take this a bit further, when you come to understand that no one knows or hears your thoughts, how then can you know what others think about you? You can't, unless of course you ask them. If you did, you might be pleasantly surprised to discover that they think you are an OK person.

Your mind is powerful. It can make or break you. You believe what you think when you have the same thought over and over again. When you have something you want to do badly, you have to put your mind into having thoughts about a successful outcome.

It's no good deciding you want to do something and yet still listen to that annoying little voice that tells you it's not possible. Incredible how often we give into that little voice, isn't it? Often it's easier to give in than to attempt to do something. Sometimes we don't want to fail again. That little voice you listen to wants to let you know it's quite at home and comfortable in it's comfort zone. It may in some weird way be trying to keep you safe, to stop you from hurting yourself, or perhaps from failing. However, when you stay strong and put aside that negative thought, decide that no matter what, you are going to give it your best shot, you might be surprised to see how easily you can succeed.

Life can be good! You have the power to be however you want. Choose to be positive. Learn how to speak and think in a positive way. Let yourself know how loved you are and what a wonderful person you are. This won't come easy when you have spent so long feeling unworthy, or not liking how things are going in your life.

Be kind to yourself. You deserve to be happy. Treat yourself with respect. Let the power you hold bubble up to the surface and overflow into your everyday life. Don't give up on yourself, stay strong and believe that you can get through what is happening in your life. Tell yourself, as often as you are able, positive things about yourself. Don't give up, strive to be better and you will. Don't listen to others who are negative towards you. Become a better person by changing your thoughts, and above all, love yourself for the wonderful person you are, and will become.

Believe this and make it so

Kay Drummond was born in England and now lives in New Zealand. She is married with a son and a daughter.

Kay has also written a personal growth book for children titled How to Be a Confident Kid.

www.ingramcontent.com/pod-product-compliance
Lightning Source LLC
Chambersburg PA
CBHW071152090426
42736CB00012B/2309